Upadesa Saram

Commentary by

P.V.S.Suryanarayana Raju

Bhagawan Sri Ramana Maharshi

Dr.P.V.S.Suryanarayana Raju.

#5-8-16, Park Street, Narsapur.

W.G.Dt, AP, INDIA.

Pin:534275.

Ph: 918814-273430.

Email: drrrajunsp@yahoo.co.in

Fax: 918814-277852.

Foreword

Upadesa is a Sanskrit word which literally means facilitating an entity to come back to its source, its home. Saram means the essence of such instruction towards that direction. The essential nature of mind is consciousness. But being covered by cloud of tendencies, past experiences, thoughts mind forgets that its nature is consciousness. This is called Self-forgetfulness.A mind that is in a state of Self-forgetfulness(Atma vismruti) leaves its source which is Self and identifies with non-Self adjuncts like the ego(Ahamkara, "I" thought),thinking process(manas)intellect(Buddhi),memory (chitta)the physical body and seeks happiness outside and in the process collects lot of misery because of conflict that is inherent in the dualistic phenomenal reality. After a break even point unable to bear this misery it starts inquiring into what is the cause of all this misery and starts investigating "who am I"," what is my nature",

" whence am i" etc. When mind uninterruptedly does this quest it existentially negates the five coverings(Pancha kosas) covering the consciousness i.e sheaths of body, vital airs(Prana)mind(manas,the thinking faculty),intellect(Buddhi, the discriminatory faculty, sheath of Self-ignorance(Anandamaya kosa)it remembers that its nature is pure conscious being. So in this way the process of bringing back the outgoing mind to its source is described in 30 Sanskrit slokas by Bhagawan Sri Ramana Maharshi which is named as Upadesa Saram by him. If his message in this properly understood it annihilates Self-ignorance and confers Self-Knowledge. Such Self-knowledge conferring books are called Darshana Grandhas in Sanskrit.Upadesa Saram is such a book. In this work the author Dr.P.V.S.Suryanarayana Raju commented on these 30 slokas of Bhagawan's Upadesa Saram

*****

About the Author

Dr.P.V.S.Suryanarayana Raju is a pediatrician from Andhra Pradesh, India, born on 12th December 1950. He has been working on the subject of self-inquiry for the past 30 years under the living Presence and guidance of Osho and Ramana Maharshi which he discovered 30 years ago in Ramanasramam. He met Osho personally in 1987 and 1989 in whose presence there happened radical transformation of being.He is a frequent visitor to Ramanasramam and out of gratefulness to Bhagawan he has written many books analyzing his teachings and these are some of them: The Art of self-enquiry, Alpha and Omega of self-inquiry, The essence of self-inquiry part 1 & 2, Insights in self-inquiry Part 1 & 2, Theory of self-inquiry, The Practice of self-inquiry, The theory and Practice of self-inquiry, The comprehensive book on self-inquiry, Know Thyself, He also wrote self-inquiry quotes in two volumes, commented on "who am I", Upadesa saram,Bhagavad Gita, self-inquiry in Bhavad Gita,

Beyond Religion, The Art of living and all are products of his own experience. He has also written many books on Self-inquiry in Telugu which include "Nenevadanu? which is a commentary of his on "who am i" in Telugu, Nija Vicharana and his most recent books in Telugu Vichara Chudamani, and Vichara Chandrodayam which mainly deal with the practical aspect of self-inquiry and he explains in them why self-inquiry is a direct and easy way for realizing the Self. He also wrote self-inquiry in Bhagavad Gita in 3 volumes, Bhagavad Gita commentary vol1, The essence of Bhagavad Gita, Beware of structure of society-it enslaves you, Gold nuggets, Inner conflict leads to outer disorder, Integral self-inquiry, Self-inquiry is the Art of comprehending the self activity, Self-inquiry is the Art of being with your Self, Self-inquiry quotes of Dr.Raju and most recently, A B C of spirituality, The genesis of self-inquiry, Self-inquiry-The science of soul, Pathless path-The Golden path of self-inquiry,

Introduction to self-inquiry, Original facelessness, Awareness-The means and goal of self-inquiry, Despair to bliss-The message of Bhagawad Gita, New man is emerging with a new way of life, Self-inquiry is the Art of being with your Self, The Sage and the scientist, and sadguru Sri Nanna garu.

*****

This book is dedicated to

Bhagawan Sri Ramana Maharshi

Eka sloki of
Bhagawan sri Ramana Maharshi.

In the middle of Heart cave there is only the Brahman.

There the consciousness is pulsating as "I am", "I am"

One can enter the heart cave and abide there either by

delving deep into the heart by self enquiry

or by stilling the vital airs.(Prana).

*****

Inquiry into the self is the most

Blissful activity of life because it

Is through which we realize the

Truth that one becomes capable of

Dropping all miseries. ~ Author
*****

Upadesa Saram

Verse1: kartur agyaya prapyathe phalam. karma kim param?
karma tat jadam.

kartur: The ordained of results. God.

agyaya: as per His orders.

prapyathe phalam: The results are obtained.

karma : the actions

kim param : Are they supreme ? [Meaning is the law of karma
the ultimate ? Who is the one who makes it happen then?]

karma tat jadam: Actions are jadam, dead lifeless entities.

Dr Raju:

*"Action is insentient. Action is not the ultimate reality so action
per se has no ability to confer the fruit of action. Fruit of
action occurs according to the whim of the ultimate reality
which is usually called God."*

Comment:

Bhagawan explains in the first verse itself why individual being performing the action is not the doer. So he is questioning the idea of doership in the first verse itself. If one understands the lie of doership the spiritual journey is over because without that lie of doership there is no existence to the thesis of ego. Ego is altered consciousness in which consciousness is mixed with adjuncts like body, thought process (manas), intellect, memory. There is superimposition of work done by adjuncts on consciousness because consciousness identifies with adjuncts and feels that adjuncts are "him". He feels separate from rest of existence. Because he identifies with adjuncts which are intrinsically limited, action proceeding from such limited entity is limited. Limited action leads to incomplete experiencing of things and so there is perennial conf;ict and contradiction with this type of action and life becomes miserable. To solve this conflict ego uses thought which is the result of psychological memory. Thought in itself is limited and its action is also limited. So the problem is much more complicated. Thought has no role to play in psychological problems. Only "insight" sees the complete map of structure of problem through perception. The awareness of movement of thought in response to problem is self-inquiry. Perception of problem in its entirety is complete action which leaves no residue of non-understanding. This is called self knowledge which is essential for complete action. Life is action in relationship and if action is not proper there is going to be conflict, contradiction, misery in life. At present we are reacting with past memories to the challenge which is always new. This incomplete action and doer ship are born out of self ignorance, it is ignorance of movement of thought and mind mechanism and it leads to mechanical way of life because action according to idea, a concept is inaction. Self ignorance is insentient so all actions born out of concept of doership are insentient because they are done in unawareness. Adjunct performing the work is not the "doer" so the fruit of action is not in his hands. In the phenomenal reality Volition(Ichha Sakti),knowledge to perform the action(Jnana Sakti),energy to perform the action(Kriya Sakti) belongs to the ultimate reality but we superimpose those qualities on us resulting in doership(Kartrutva) and enjoyership(Bhoktrutva) anomalies. Action has no ability to confer the bliss which is not of this world. So action is not the ultimate reality.

When Sun shines the lotus blooms. Then who is responsible for this blooming. Blooming is happening occurring in the presence of Sun light. So neither the Sun nor the lotus are the doers of this happening. It is a natural law that lotus blooms in Sun light. It is in the nature of things. But mind tries to conceptualize natural events in it's language and says either Sun is the doer or lotus is the doer. If we closely scrutinize this logic it will be found that there is no doer at all, things happen as naturally as they should be. Mind always tries to translate the things that which it does not know into it's language of known by conceptualizing. Concept has no substance in it and reality asserts itself. Bhagawan is telling what is real in the sphere of action and the limitations of action in this first verse and the futility of doing actions thinking that they yield results according to their expectation and wish.

*****

Verse2: Kriti mahodadhou patana karanam phalam ashashvatam gati nirodhakam.

kriti - maha - udau : The vast ocean of actions
patana karanam: is the cause for fall [spiritual fall]
phalam ashashvatam: The result is transient.
gati nirodhakam: acts to stop spiritual progress.

The reason for someone's not progressing in spiritual path is getting lost in the ocean of actions.

Verse 2:

"Vast Ocean of actions cause us to fall from uninterrupted blissful self awareness which is our natural state to mere object knowing consciousness and result of the action is transient and obstruct our goal to posit the mind in the Pure conscious being."

Comment:

To be in a state of bliss is inherent in every human being. When he forgets the blissful nature of his self he tries to gain happiness through actions which cause comfort to the body and which satisfy the psychological needs of the mind. In the pursuit of happiness he indulges in actions which may give him pleasure which is always transient and always associated with the shadow of misery. Pleasure and pain are always together in the result of action. Any form of action involves seeming movement of attention away from the self whose nature is bliss, towards an object which does not have the property of bliss intrinsically. So the pursuit of pleasure which is the result of self ignorance involves action which obstruct the recognition of our natural state of blissful self awareness. Actions always leads to formation of tendencies which obstruct our natural state of self conscious being.

*****

Verse 3: ishvara-arpitam na ichaya kritam , chitta shodakam mukti sadhakam.

ishvararpitam: Dedicated to God.
na ichaya kritam: not desiring.
Chitta shodakam: purifies the mind
mukti sadanam: is an aid to liberation.

Dedicating the results of action to God and not desiring leads to purification of mind and this practise is an aid to liberation.

Verse 3:
"When work is done without doership or desire and fruit of work is devoted to God mind is purified to the state of suddha Manas which helps us
to get liberated from the apparent imprisonment in the ego which is a creation of thought."

Comment:

There is relation between work and the ego. Our attitude(Bhavana) towards the result of action is very important. By birth any human being is born with tendencies and desires. When work is born out of desire there is always an eye on the fruit of work. When there is an eye on fruit of action "doer" is born. Doer is not an existential entity. Because we do work with an eye on the fruit of work "doer appears to exist" because of continuous flow of thought that he is the doer. Suppose if an electrical bulb is rotated circularly with certain velocity the bulb appears as a circle of fire which in reality does not exist. Similarly continuous thought doer-ship make us to believe that it is an existential entity.

Doership is just an idea born only when work is done with desire with an eye to enjoy the fruit of action (Kartrutva,Bhoktrutva Bhranthi) so when we devote the fruit of work to God the idea of doer and doership will not be there, and once there is no doership there is no ego. In this way impersonal activity purifies the mind by getting rid of idea of doership which prepares the mind to reflect Pure consciousness thus paving the way for liberation. Dispassion must be there before doing the action, during the action and after the action when fruit of action is conferred. If there is no dispassion action is contaminated with the idea of doership. So impersonal action is a great aid for liberation. We should not renounce doing action but we should renounce idea of doer-ship and an eye on the fruit of action. Lord Krishna stressed in Bhagavat Gita about this attitude towards the work and the fruit of work. Work done with desire and doership binds and limits our consciousness (kinchigna), where as impersonal work helps us to get liberated from the shackles of ego.

*****

Verse 4: kaya vang manah karyam uttamam pujanam japat chintanam krama

kaya-vak-manah: with body, speach and mind

karyam: acts

pujanam: worship

japa: chanting

chintanam: contemplation

kramat: order

uttama: better

"worship,japa,contemplation are the best activities in that order ... performed respectively with body,speech and mind."

Upadesha Saram Verse 4:

"Rituals done by the body, repetition of a sacred word, prayer, singing in the name of God done by the voice, self-enquiry done by the mind are effective in cleansing the mind and their effect of cleansing increases in that order i.e. self-enquiry is more effective than Japa, and Japa is more effective than rituals."

Comment:

Bhagawan is telling various methods to be adopted to clean the mind and their effectiveness in this verse. We are aware of three states of waking, dreaming, deep sleep states. But there is fourth state of mind also which is called Turiya when mind in its pure state when mind is empty of the contents. Fourth state of mind is filled with awareness only. To recognize fourth state purity of mind is necessary. Rituals are gross form of worship done by the gross body. Ritual is not a goal in itself but an aid to spiritual progress. In devotion there is the surrender of the ego so mental activity is reduced which finally leads to the extinction of the ego. If we stop giving energy to the ego, the ego dies it's natural death. Rituals, repetition of a sacred word and self-enquiry stop the energy from feeding the ego; instead they divert our energy and attention Self wards. If we stop attending to the ego by whatever be the method, ego become tenuous and finally it loses its hold on us and later it will die a natural death. Ego is Self consciousness "I am" with adjuncts. It identifies not only with the adjuncts like body, thought process, intellect, and memory but also the self consciousness "I am". Mind is the identifying agent. It identifies with anything for security because it knows the transiency of thought. It wants something permanent in terms of time, so it invents god, nirvana, moksha. Our aim is to separate Self consciousness from mixing with the adjuncts by nullifying the identifying agency which is ego. If there is no identity of Self consciousness with the adjuncts there is no place for ego to exist.

Rituals, Japa, self-enquiry aids in nullifying the identifying agency and their effect of nullification is more in the order of rituals, Japa, self-enquiry. In self-enquiry the ego structure and mechanics are understood and we go beyond grip of ego and our attention is paid only to the source of the ego and awareness falls on itself which is Self realization. So in self-enquiry ego is attended to, but we do not give energy by identifying with it, so ego dries up because of lack of energy supply and one day it falls altogether. This is called Self realization because self consciousness disidentifies itself from the imagining as mere adjuncts and Self consciousness is left in it's pure form. Prayer, singing the Lord's greatness are part of action done by the voice in the service of God. So we have to do service to God with the three instruments of body, voice and mind to get rid of the identifying agency which is tying Self consciousness with the adjuncts and thus creating innumerable troubles arising out of this wrong identity. So self knowledge is important in life because we do not identify with anything if we have self knowledge. In this way our mind is cleansed of the contaminants of thought matter in psyche effectively. Then we have empty mind (Amanaska sthithi), a mind devoid of contents like ideas, dogmas, degenerating factors which cause continuous leak of energy, tendencies which compel us to do self centered activity. Empty mind has the capacity to comprehend that which is eternal in us. Mind is a reflecting medium and it shows the presence of contents if they are there and it also mirrors pure consciousness if we are devoid of any contents.

*****

verse5: Jagata ishadi yuka sevanam, ashtamurthi vrid daiva pujanam.

jagatah sevanam: serving the world

ishadi yukta: treating it as a manifestation of God.

ashta-murthi-vrid: consisting of eight fold form

deva pujanam: prayer to God.

worshiping the eight fold form of God and serving the world treating it as a manifestation of God is proper worship.

Upadesha Saram Verse 5:

"To serve the world looked upon as the manifestation of the Lord, is to offer worship to the Lord of eight fold forms. "

Comment:

Lord is omniscient so he pervades every atom of his creation. Creation is the adjunct of Lord i.e. Eswara. Earth, water, fire, air, ether, Sun, Moon and all living beings are eight fold manifestation of the Lord. Space happens due to Pancha Bhutas (Five fundamental elements of creation) and Time happens due to the presence of Sun and the Moon. All Jivas (Beings with adjuncts) function in the purview of time and space. They have no independent existence beyond time and space. So worship of these eight fold forms regarded all as forms of his, is perfect worship of Lord. This type of worship is without doership and there is surrender in it, so it purifies the mind and paves the way for self realization. When we see the world with this Bhavana we will feel that we are seeing and serving the Lord. Such type of devotion is called Para Bhakti. Sri Rama Krishna Parama Hamsa used to see Mother Kali in everything. For saint Nami Nandi Adigal every one in Tiruvur used to appear as Siva to him. This is Para Bhakti.

*****

verse 6: uttama stavad ucha mandatah chitajam japa-dyananam uttamam

uttama -- superior or better

stavat - than stuti or singing glories

ucha (japa) - loud japa

mandatah - softer (japa)

chittajam (japa) --- japa in mind

japa dyanam - japa that is automatic form, inward --literally mental japa

uttamam - is the best

Upadesa Saram Verse 6:

"Better than the best hymns of devotional praise is the repetitive uttering of sacred names in which uttering with low voice(upamsu japa) is better than uttering louder(uchha japa),but best of all is the meditation in the mind(mental japa)."

Comment:

Describing the greatness of Lord in detail is the best devotional praise. It is better for japa to be done in low voice than loud voice. The aim of japa is to hold on to a single thought thus excluding all other thoughts. As japa progresses mind will be subdued and mind becomes one pointed (Ekagra chitta) and to such a mind, silence of the Self conscious being is revealed which is usually called self knowledge. Japa withdraws our attention from the nonself and withdrawing of attention from nonself amounts to attending to the Self conscious being because awareness falls on itself. Once we learn this skill of abiding and holding on to pure consciousness spiritual progress becomes easy and effortless. Japa should be done with passionate devotion to the truth but not mechanically. Japa should be done with total self surrender (Poorna saranagathi) to have good results. Once we exclude attending to nonself what remains is only the "Self" and to rest in and as Self is the aim of all spiritual disciplines.

*****

verse 7: Ajya dharaya srotasa samam sarala chintanam viralatah param.

sarala chintanam: continuous [firmly established, without breaks] abidance as[on] Self.
viralatah : interupted
param: is superior. [meaning continuous abidance is better than abidance with breaks].

ajya dharaya srotasa samam: like a river; a continuous flow of Ghee.

Upadesa Saram Verse 7:

"Like an unbroken flow of oil or a stream of water, continuous meditation is better than which is interrupted."

Comment:
Deliberate meditation is mental activity and is always interrupted by thought disturbance due to the influence of innate tendencies. "Me" is the result of desire which itself is dependent on object seen by senses. So "me" is built on sensate value only. "Me" is the result of evolution of body-mind complex and so "me" is time. So "me" is non-Self, so is time. Ego is commonly interested in indulging in sense enjoyment because it thrives on non-Self and such a mind has to be prepared to be one pointed through rituals, Japa, meditation and enquiry. Then mind is gradually emptied of its contents and such a mind has the capacity to meditate without interruption and its attention moves Self wards without any break. Continuous Self ward flow of mind is easy for those who withdraw their attention from nonself and abide in Self and be as Self without any separative feeling. Such a mind is called Atmakara or Brahmakara vritti. This is the goal of all spiritual disciplines

*****

Verse 8: bheda bhavanat soham ityasau bhavana bhida pavani mata

bheda bhavanat : (superior) to contemplation with duality is

Bhavana abhida: contemplation without duality.
sah aham iti : That "He is me"
asau: This (contemplation without duality)

pavani mata: considered as purifier of mind.

Contemplation without duality that "He is me" is considered as greater purifier of mind than that which is based on duality.

Upadesa Saram Verse 8:
"Meditation on the identity of Individual (jiva) and the Lord (Eswara), "I am He" is more purifying than meditation which assumes a difference between them."

Comment:
Ego is basically finite consciousness. It is Self consciousness "I am" mixed and identified with adjuncts, beliefs, ideas, nationality, caste, creed, race, profession etc. So ego is an affirmation of separateness. Separative feeling is a mirage created by the ego.

The idea of separative feeling is apparent only in the dimension of time and space. The idea of separativeness veils the truth. Separative feeling is a hindrance to spiritual growth. Ego takes shelter in the false idea of being the body and it feels separate from Godliness by contrasting itself with other forms of life. Ego being finite can know only finite things. Ego believe that God and the world to be separate from itself. It reduces God to something being finite. Anything that is separate from anything else is limited and thus necessarily finite. So long as we experience ourselves as a limited individual we feel God is a being who is distinct and separate from us. We limit the infinity of God.

If we know or experience God as anything other than our own essential Self, we are not experiencing him "as he really is" but only as mind made vision (Manomayamam katchi).Though God is visible when we worship him with a separative feeling and there is cleansing and purification of the mind of it's desire and attachment to worldly pleasures, there is still mistaken experience that we are finite and we are separate from God. Trotapuri removed this type of mistaken experience of Sri Ramakrishna Paramahamsa by conferring him nondual experience of the Self.

The only way to experience the Self is by being it. Literally we cannot experience Self, there is only experiencing. Being as we are is the only means by which we can experience the absolute reality "as it is". So meditating without separative feeling with strong conviction of "I am He" is superior to meditating with assumption that God is separate from us. With this type meditation of identity of individual (jiva) and the Lord (Eswara) there is disintegration of the ego ending in realizing the Truth.

*****

Verse 9: Bhava sunyasad bhava susthitih bhavana balad bhaktir uttama

Bhavana balat : based upon the strenghth of thought [ie, i am he]

sad bhava sustitih: (the meditator gains) firm abidance in the Self.

Bhava sunya : independent of thoughts

Bhaktir uttamam: This is supreme devotion.

Upadesa Saram Verse 9:

"By the power of meditation, devoid of thoughts one is established in true being, and this is supreme devotion."

Comment:

The "I" thought (I-am-the-body-idea) arises from the spiritual heart centre, raises to the brain and identifies with the body and imagines itself to be the body." I-am-the-body" is the primal imagination that thinks all other thoughts. So if we want to be free of thoughts we must be free from "I-am-the-body-idea". The "I" thought creates an illusion that there is a mind or individual Self (Kinchijna) which inhabits the body and directs all thoughts and actions. The "I" thought accomplishes this by identifying itself with all thoughts and perceptions of the mind. The idea that one is an individual person is generated and sustained by "I" thought and by it's habit of constantly attaching itself to all the thoughts that arise. If one can break the connection between" I" thought and the thoughts it identifies with them through self-enquiry the "I" thought is deprived of all the thoughts and perceptions that it normally identifies with, then the "I" thought itself will subside and finally disappear. This can be done by holding on to "I" thought and excluding all other thoughts. If one can keep attention on the inner feeling of "I"
we can hold on to "I" thought, then it will start to subside into the spiritual heart centre. Through self-enquiry when we free our mind of all thoughts except the "I" thought, the magnetic power of Self pulls the "I" thought back into the heart centre culminating in the collapse and eventually the "I" thought is destroyed completely and never raises again. When this happens the idea of individual Self is destroyed, only Self remains. This is Bhava sunya sadbhava susthiti. This is supreme devotion says Bhagawan.

*****

Verse 10: hasthale manah svasthata kirya Bhakti yoga Bodhasca nischitam

manah svasthata : abidance of mind

hrt sthale : in the heart.

kriya bhakti:yoga of action

yoga bodhah cha: devotion, astanga yoga and yoga of knowledge.

nischitam: it is determined.

Upadesa Saram Verse 10:

"Having subsided in the place of rising in one's own source of real self is an action (karma) without desire, Bhakti (devotion),that is Yoga (union with God), Jnana (true knowledge)."

Comment:

A conscious particle from the spiritual heart enters the brain and when it identifies with the body it becomes the "I "thought and creates the illusion of individual self which inhabits the body and identifies itself with all thoughts and perceptions. Upadesa literally means bringing back a thing to it's place of origin or source. So the goal of self-enquiry is to bring back this conscious particle which is straying with the help of adjuncts in the nonSelf to its source which is spiritual heart. Self-inquiry reverses the process of" I" thought getting identified with all other thoughts and perceptions of daily life as separate entity. If one can break the connection between "I" thought and thoughts and perceptions it identifies with, then the "I" thought itself will subside and finally disappear. This can be done by holding on to "I" thought i.e. inner feeling of "I" or "I am" and excluding all other thoughts. If one can keep attention to the inner feeling of "I" then this conscious particle dissociates from the adjuncts. Then the power of Self pulls the "I" thought back into the heart centre and eventually destroys it so completely that it never raises again. When this happens the concept of individual Self is destroyed once and forever, only Self remains. Thus mind remains subsided in the source of real Self from which it has risen takes the form of Atmakara Vritti and that is the culminating point of Karma Yoga (the path of desire less action),Bhakti Yoga (The path of devotion) Raja Yoga with the methods of mind control and the Jnana Yoga (the path of knowledge through self-enquiry, atma vichara).

*****

Summary of first ten verses of Upadesa Saram:

Bhagawan's method of destroying the concept of individual Self which is usually called as manonasa or destruction of the mind is scientific and unlike in other methods which are dependent on thought which itself is product of self ignorance, uses awareness in bringing back the conscious particle that is apparently imprisoned in ego and it's tendencies, to it's (the conscious particle) source of spiritual heart and make it to permanently abide there so that it never rises as ego again. In this way his approach to Truth is non-traditional and the outlook is above beyond all religions and it is relevant to entire humanity irrespective of their religious background. What is required here is intense and passionate longing for Truth and it will lead us to the truth if we do self-enquiry with such a passion as a drowning man struggles for air. However even though his approach is non-traditional, he never condemned tradition and instead made best use of it by utilizing it for the preparation of the mind for making it fit to do self-enquiry. In this endeavour he integrated Karma, Bhakti, Raja and Jnana yogas. In the first ten verses of Upadesa Saram he described in detail how Karma Yoga and Bhakti Yoga aid in Self-abidance.

Every human being is born with self-ignorance. So he has defects (doshas) of

1) Doer-ship which results in action with desire with eye on the fruit of desire (sakama karma)

2) vibhakti (devotion to his real Self with separative feeling, i.e. God)

3)Viyoga (the feeling of separation from the rest other than his body-mind complex and so he feels that the world is separate and contrary to him and he feels that God is apart from him.4)Ignorance (not knowing the nature of his Self. Because I am confining myself to summarize first 10 verses I will elaborate only on kama yoga and Bhakti yoga with relevance to Bhagawan's teaching in Upadesa Saram. All these defects occur to "I" thought only.

Karma Yoga to relieve the dosha of sakama karma:- In sakama karma there is the sense of doership with an eye on the fruit of action.

Sakama karma is an attempt to gain happiness in nonself, so sakama karma is born out of Self-ignorance. Self-ignorance is insentient so sakama karma is insentient, jada and so it has no ability to direct or confer the fruit of action. The performer of the work is not the doer and so fruit of action is not in his hands .Fruit of action perishes by enjoying it as pleasure or pain. But having perished thus the fruit of that action will still remain in the seed form as liking to do such an action again and this is called tendency. So tendencies result from action with doership which encourages us for further action thus throwing us into the sea of actions which obstructs our spiritual goal and we are lost in the sea of actions. So sakama karma is Patana karanam (Action arising from ego leads to fall away from Self) and Gati nirodhakam (keeps us away from self knowledge).So as an antidote to dosha of sakama karma Bhagawan is advising us not indulge in action and to do work expected from you without any desire, without eye on fruit of action, without doership, to offer the fruit of action to God with surrender so that sense of doership is nullified. This type of nishkama karma (Action without an end in view) purifies the mind and it is an aid to keep the mind subsided in it's source.

Bhakti yoga:- Average human being is more devoted to the

whims and fancies of his ego and tendencies and usually prays to God to fulfill them rather than to his true self because he is self-ignorant. Even sakama puja, japa, dhyana does not purify the mind because the ego is strengthened in these in the name of devotion. Puja, japa, dhyana are actions done by organs of body, speech, mind and they should be done without sense of doership or desire, expectation, goal if the mind were to be purified. So devotion must also be desire less(nishkama) so that mind is purified. If this is done with ananya bhava (I am he) the meditator himself becomes nonexistent by merging in the state of being It is beyond the comprehension of thought and thought is not there in that state and is called Bhavanatita sadbhava susthiti.

In no mind state "I" thought loses it's identity with the body, thoughts, sense perception and becomes conscious of the body, in contrast to body identity previously he had.. Because there is no identity with anything Pure "I" thought is not binding as a burnt rope is not binding as you rightly said. The beauty of no mind state is that it reflects the light of awareness of Pure consciousness even when we are engaged in work in the phenomenal reality. Bhagawan said no mind state is "Self" itself for all practical purposes. Actually mind is insentient and we are imposing life upon it and animating it. Withdrawing that life force which we have imposed on the mind is the goal of spiritual sadhana.

*****

Verse 11:
vayurodhanat liyyathe manah jalapakshivat rodhasadhanam

vayurodhanat : by restrain of the prana
manah : the mind
liyate : becomes absorbed
jala pakshivat: like the ensnaring of the bird
rodha sadhanam: is a means of checking

By holding the breath, mind is restrained like a bird caught in a net. This is a way to restrain the distracted mind.

Upadesa Saram Verse 11:
"The mind may be subdued by regulating the breath, just as a bird is restrained when caught in a net."

Comment:

Pranayama is the science of breath. Mind is accustomed to stray in nonself leaving its source the "Self". To control such a chaotic mind cultivating the prana (life force) makes the mind temporarily settled like a pond in full moon light and mind for the first time tastes the bliss and happiness of thought free state while awake. This tasting of bliss makes the aspirant certain that the nature of his being is bliss. So he pursues further to establish in that state of bliss without any interruption. In this way pranayama is an aid in preparing the mind of the aspirant to do self-enquiry. In pranayama only manolaya (temporary cessation of activity of the mind) happens and so annihilation of tendencies will not happen in pranayama. No radical transformation of the mind is possible in pranayama. It helps us to taste the bliss of thoughtless state of the mind as long as pranayama lasts. Prnayama is an important Anga in Astanga Yoga. Body health and quality and length of life are profoundly affected positively due to pranayama. But when the breath (prana) comes out, the mind will also come out and wander under the sway of tendencies as usual. So pranayama is mere aid for restraining the mind but will not bring destruction of the mind.

*****

Quote
Verse 12:

citta vayavas chit-kriya-yutah sakhayor-dvyai sakti mulaka

chitta-vayavah : the mind and the vital airs
cit kriya yutah: they are endowed with consciousness and the
activising force.
sakhayoh dvayi: they are the two branches

sakti mulaka: the root cause of energy or power

The mind and the vital airs are the two branches with thought
and action as functions that eminate from the same root.

Upadesa Saram Verse 12:
*"Mind and breath manifesting in thought and action, branch
out from a common source, Atma Sakti (Aham Spurana)."*

Comment:

The mind is the conscious aspect, the power of objective knowing, thinking (Jnana Sakti) where as breath or life force (Prana) is the power of doing or action (kriya sakti).But the original power Aham Sphurana is like a trunk of a tree having mind and prana as two branches. So mind and prana are interrelated. The imaginary power of the mind comes to a stand still if breath is controlled. Likewise if mind stops imagining completely whatever is the reason breath comes to a standstill. Prana supplies energy to mind for thinking and to the body for it's maintenance. When mind is strayed if we control the breath, immediately it feels suffocated, stops imagining and comes back to the present. If due to self-enquiry thought process collapses in the spiritual heart the breath is controlled. The existence of the mind depends upon it's identity with something gross. In self-enquiry because we pay our entire attention on the source of mind identity with nonself including all adjuncts is nullified, so attraction to nonself does not exist and in such a state of being there is direct experience of nonexistence of the mind (naiva manasam).The ego, the thinker appears as a real entity because of our continuous identity with the nonself. This identity is broken when we pay attention only to "I" thought excluding all other thoughts. Then "I" thought is deprived of it's identity with all other thoughts and perceptions it normally identifies with. Then the "I" thought start to subside in the spiritual heart and gets dissolved in it.

*****

Verse 13: laya vinashane ubhaya rodhane laya gatham punar
bhavati no-mrutam

laya vinashane : absorption and destruction
ubhaya rodhane : by the restrain of both [prana and mind]
laya gatam : (the mind) that has gone to absorption
punar: again
bhavati na: does not come into existence
mritam: having died.

Upadesa Saram Verse 13:

"Absorption or laya, destruction or nasa are the two kinds of mind control. When merely absorbed, it emerges again, but not when it is destroyed."

Comment:

Subsidence of mind is two kinds. Abeyance (laya) and destruction (nasa).That which is in abeyance will rise but if mind dies it will not rise. The subsidence of mind is gained by breath restraint and in states like sleep, death, swoon, coma is temporary and is thus manolaya or abeyance of the mind. Since happiness is experienced only when the mind subsides and since rising of the mind is misery itself, if we are to enjoy happiness forever it is necessary that the mind is destroyed permanently. Such permanent destruction of the mind which is the true goal of all spiritual disciplines is called manonasa. The reason why breath control cannot bring about manonasa is breath control does not destroy the tendencies.

For making the mind subside permanently there is no adequate means other than self-enquiry. If made to subside by other means, the mind will remain as if subsided but will definitely rise again. Where as in manonasa (destruction of the mind) the "I" thought is pulled into the spiritual heart centre which eventually destroys it so completely that it never rises again. The concept of individual self is destroyed forever, only Self remains.

*****

Verse 14:
Prana bandhanat lina manasam eka cintanat nasam etyadah

pranama bandanat: by controlling the breath
lina manasam : the mind becomes absorbed
adah : this
eka cintanat by contemplation on the one Truth
nasham iti : this goes to destruction

Upadesa Saram Verse 14:

"When the mind has been suspended by breath restraint, it may then be annihilated by single minded attention (Eka chintana) to the self."

Comment:

When one makes the mind which has subsided by restraining the breath, go on the path of knowing i.e self-enquiry and becoming one with the self and it's form will die. Self-enquiry is not only the path of knowing and becoming the Self but is also one and the only path which will destroy the mind. When mind activity is ceased and mind becomes one pointed due to breath restraint, it should keenly scrutinize and know pure conscious being in the heart which is adjunct less and thought excluding. So one should make use of that peaceful state gained by Pranayama by turning one's attention to scrutinize and know the real import of "I", then mind will die, for it will be known that there is no such thing as mind at all. In self-enquiry there is annihilation of tendencies leading to no mind (amanaska) state. The mind rests in pure self conscious being without straying because the tendencies are annihilated.

Here is a state of mind in which there is only the perception of "what is" without naming it. This happens in Amanaska sthiti in which mind is filled only with awareness without any noise of the past. Some. Pure Ahamkara Vritti is there even in Jnanis (suddha manas) because,idamkara vritti is not possible without Ahamkara vritti.

*****

Verse 15:

nasta manasah utkrsta yoginah krtyam asi kim svasthitim yatah

nasta manasah: one the mind (identification) is destroyed

utkrsta yoginah: for such exalted Yogis

krtyam asi kim: what is there to be done ?

svastitim yahah: revel in one's natural state

Upadesa Saram Verse 15:

Meaning:
"What action remains to be done by that great yogi whose mind has been extinguished and who rests in his own true and transcend state of being?"

Comment:

For the one whose mind is destroyed and who abides in the Self has no doership, no desires, no tendencies there is not action left for him to do. He no longer mistakes himself to be the body-mind complex, so does not associates himself with the fruit of action, free of all tendencies, Self absorbed. One, whose mind is destroyed is greatest in the existence. His mind becomes one with the self and always enjoys the bliss of self without any interruption. Just the presence of their silent being transforms the whole world. The original nature of the mind is
consciousness but when it associates with the adjuncts, volition (desire, will, sankalpa) and doubt(vikalpa) arise in it. When the mind dissociates from the adjuncts there is destruction of sankalpa (desire) vikalpa (doubt) vritti (modification of the mind) is destroyed. In religious jargon it is called manonasa or destruction of the mind.Such a great one (utkrusta) enjoys the bliss of self which is revealed spontaneously because of the destruction of the concept of individual self and there is no single thing exists for him to do. He does not know any other thing than self. Whatever action he may appear to do exist only in the outlook who mistake him to be the body which does the action.
So from 11th to 15th verse Bhagawan dealt in detail about Raja yoga, so he alloted first fifteen verses on how karma, Bhakti, Raja yoga helps in preparing an aspirant for self-enquiry and in the rest of the verses Bhagawan taught the path of self-enquiry i.e Jnana Marga.(Path of knowledge)

Having prepared the mind of the aspirant by directing the awareness of the mind and actions of the body Self wards through karma, Bhakti, Yoga which involve the dynamic aspect of the self i.e body-mind complex, now it is the right time to hold on to conscious aspect of the self. So Bhagawan teaches method of self-enquiry from 16th verse to 19th verse.

*****

Verse 16: drishya varathim cittam atmanah citva darshanam tattva darshanam

cittam: mind
drishya varitim : having withdrawn from the objects, the seen
atmanah : of its own: Self
citva sarshanam : vision of the consciousness
tatva darshanam: the vision of the Reality

Upadesa Saram Verse 16:

"If one's attention is turned away from external objects of sense perception and focused on the light of self, that is the true vision of reality.(Atmanusandhana of mind)."

Comment:
Wise people observe the phenomenal reality "as it is" and recognize without doubt that any attempt in indulging in the affairs of nonself definitely leads to misery. Lord Krishna in Bhagavad Gita mentioned that world is a temple of misery (Dhukhalaya). If we enter into that temple misery will be conferred on us. The way of life of humanity is miserable because majority indulge in nonself and they feel individual existence is a reality and they are confident that anything can be achieved by their own effort. They are not aware that one higher power is responsible for the affairs of the world and events are happening through them but not because of them. If one realizes this, naturally he loses interest in nonself and his attention falls back on itself which amounts to seeing it's own nature of consciousness. Thus mind knowing that it's nature is awareness only, gives up object knowing attitude, this alone is seeing of the reality (Tattwa darsanam).

The "I" thought superimposes afflictions and pleasures of body and mind on it and says,i am suffering from a disease instead of saying my body is suffering from disease,and at the mental level it says i am miserable or happy instead of saying my mind feels miserable or happy. This type of language continues as long as the habit of identity to body-mind complex continues.

It is the silent awareness that reads, breaths, listens etc but the "I" thought comes in between the body and self and claims the doership of the activities. "I" thought is an altered state of consciousness but it has within it the essential pure consciousness in it's core. So instead of seeking enlightenment it if we focus our attention on "I" thought, the real "I" reveals itself

which is behind the "I" thought and is the basis of "I' thought. This is real self-enquiry.

*****

Quote

Verse 17: manasam tu kim margane krite naiva manasam marga arja vat

kim manasam: what is mind ?

margane krite : inquiring thus

na eva manasam: there is no mind

marga arja vat: This is the direct path

Upadesa Saram Verse 17:

"Again, if one persists in enquiring, "what is this mind of mine" it will be found that there is no such thing as "mind". This is the direct path."

Comment:

In this verse Bhagawan shows the way how the mind is to know it's own form of light. When we scrutinize the mind i.e. personality it will be found that there is no such thing as ego or personality. Enquiry is not a thought but paying attention to it. There is no ego apart from the idea of it. Ego is psychological memory, an aberration on the pure Self born out of body identity. The conscious aspect of the ego arises from the Self and in fact the Self but forgetful of it's nature because of it's association with the adjuncts and it believes in the lie of it's separate independent existence. When we focus our attention on the source of the ego it's lie of it's independent existence is revealed and as we practice like this with such an intensity as drowning man struggles for air, the lie is extinguished forever and the concept of individual self is annihilated and only self remains. What was appearing as the mind is nothing but Self, the Pure consciousness "I am". Existence consciousness is the sole reality of the unreal mind. In self-enquiry pure consciousness remains, only limitations become extinct.

*****

Quote

Verse 18: Vrtta yas tvaham vrttim asritah vrttayo mano viddhyaham manah

vrtta yah : thoughts as they

aham vrittim: the "I" thought

ashritah: depend

vriyah manah: thoughts in the mind

viddhi may u know

aham manah : i thought is the mind

Upadesa Saram Verse 18:

"The mind is only multitude of thoughts. Of all these thoughts, the "I" thought, the feeling of "I-am-the-body" is the root. Therefore what is called mind is the root thought "I"."

Comment:
"I" thought is one thread on which all other thoughts are strung and since no other thought can exist in it's absence, therefore what is commonly called mind is the root thought "I-am-the-body" idea. "I" thought is the mixed feeling of "I-am-the-body". Real "I" is the Pure existence "I am". The "I" thought is the knowing subject, where as all other thoughts are objects known by it. Hence, though other thoughts come and go,"I" thought always remains as the background upon which they depend and when "I" thought subsides, all other thoughts must subside along with it. Thus "I" thought is the one and only characteristic of the mind. Therefore ultimate truth about the mind can be discovered only when one scrutinizes the truth of the first person "I" thought.

The "I" thought is a superimposition on real "I'. The core of "I" thought is pure consciousness. So when we scrutinize the "I" thought and if one can keep attention on the inner feeling of "I', then the "I" thought start to subside into the heart centre i.e pure consciousness. This can be done by holding on to inner feeling of "I am" excluding all other thoughts. "I" thought is an altered state of consciousness in which consciousness is associated with adjucts and there arises a compound consciousness which is basically object knowing consciousness where as basic form of consciousness is exclusive self consciousness (Real "I",thaan,"I""I") in which awareness is aware of itself only, while consciousness associated with adjuncts is aware of objects.(False "I",nan,) But in both the cases that which cognises is only Pure consciousness. There are no two separate conscious entities, one for knowing objective reality and another for knowing itself. Our being itself is Self conscious, Self effulgence.

Quote

Verse 19: aham ayam kutau bhavati chinvatah ayi patatyaham nija vicharanam

kutah: from where ?

ayam: this

aham: I thought

Bhavati: comes to existence

cinvatah: the conscious person who does this inquiry

ayi: Oh!

aham patati : the "I" falls

nija vicharanam: Through this self inquiry

Upadesa Saram Verse 19:

"When one scrutinizes with in thus, "what is the rising place of "I"?,the "I" thought will subside(die). This is self-enquiry (Jnana Vichara)."

Comment:
When one inwardly scrutinizes root thought, the feeling "I-am-the-body" in order to find out from where it arises, it will subside and disappear because, like the snake in the rope it has no reality of it's own and hence appear to exist only when it is not keenly scrutinized. This vigilant inward scrutiny of "I" thought, alone is Jnana Vichara, the enquiry which leads to true self knowledge.

*****

Verse 20: ahami nasha bhajyahamahamtaya spurthi hrt-svayam param punya sat

ahami nasa bhiji : when the ahamkara is destroyed

svayam : to its own

hrt: The heart

param purna : The Supreme Completeness

sphurti : Shines forth

aham-aham: as "I" - "I"

Upadesa Saram Verse 20:

"In the place where "I" i.e the mind or ego merges, the one (Existence consciousness, basic form of consciousness) appears spontaneously as "I" "I" or "I am I". That it is the whole (Poorna)."

Comment:
When the mind or the ego, the feeling of "I am this" or "I am that" subsides and merges in it's source, the real Self, the one true existence consciousness shines forth spontaneously as "I" "I" or " I am I"(Thaan), devoid of all superimposed adjuncts such as "this" or "that". This adjunct-less "I" "I" is the self, the absolute reality, the whole (Poorna).Bhagawan says that as a result of such self-enquiry, the reality will shine forth spontaneously as "I" "I" or "I am I".

*****

Quote

Verse 21: idam aham pada bhikhyam anvaham ahami linake aip alaya satta ya

idam: This (Self)
aham pada: the root of "I"
abhikhyam: Ego, I word.
anu: following
aham: The Source of I
ahami linake : the merger of I
Alaya Satta ya : As the Source is Indestructable Truth itself

Upadesa Saram Verse 21:

The "I" "I", the whole is always the import of word "I" because we exist even deep sleep ,which is devoid of "I" thought i.e mind. Since we do not become nonexistent even in deep sleep, where the mind in the form of "I-am-the-body" does not exist and since we are conscious of our existence in deep as "I am", that one reality which shines forth as "I" "I" or "I am I" when the mind merges in it's source and dies, is always in all the three states of waking, dreaming, deep sleep and in all three times i.e the past, present and the future~ the true import of word "I".

*****

Quote

Verse 22: vigrah -indriyah prana dhi tamah naham eka sat
tajjadam hi asah

vigrah: form
indriyah: (made up of) sense organs
prana: breath (mind)
dhi: intellect
tamah: ignorance(vasanas/deep sleep seath)
tat jadam: are all inert [Dead entities]
aham eka sat : i am none of these.
hi asat: ( ) indeed non-existent
na: not.

Upadesa Saram Verse 22:

*"Since the body, mind, intellect, breath and darkness of
ignorance which remains in deep sleep are all insentient
(Jada) and unreal (Asat),they are not "I" which is the reality."*

Comment:
Bhagawan is negating the five sheaths (Pancha kosas) which
apparently cover the consciousness because they are
insentient and unreal, because they do not possess inherent
consciousness or existence of their own. Hence they cannot
be the "I", the reality which is both self existing and self
shining. The feeling of "I" is mixed up with adjuncts, so
Bhagawan is negating the adjuncts to show the true import of
"I" which is the reality.
The five sheaths are:-
   1) Physical body~ Annamaya kosa.
   2) Breath or life force~ Pranamaya kosa.
   3) The mind~ Manomaya kosa.
   4) The intellect~ Vijnanamaya kosa.
   5) The darkness of ignorance~ Anandamaya kosa which is
      experienced in deep sleep due to disappearance of

other four sheaths.

By means of sequence of ideas presented in verses 16-22 Bhagawan reveals us the true and practical import of scriptural teaching "neti, neti"(not this, not this).Traditionally neti, neti is done as an intellectual method. Einstein says that a problem cannot be solved on the same level of consciousness that gave rise to the problem which means the problem of self-ignorance cannot be solved by effort of it's progeny of five sheaths.

Bhagawan reveals that neti,neti is not intended to denote a method of practice but only indicates a final state of experience which is different in the level and quality of consciousness compared to the present altered state of consciousness with the association of adjuncts.

In verses 16-19 Bhagawan teaches us the method of practicing self-enquiry.

In the verse 20 he teaches us that as a result of such practice the reality will shine forth spontaneously as "I""I" or " I am I".

In the verse 21 he declares that the reality which thus shines forth as "I" "I" is always the true import of "I".

And finally in verse 22 he concludes by saying that since the five sheaths are insentient and unreal, they cannot be "I", the reality whose nature is existence consciousness.

So true knowledge that the five sheaths are not "I" is an experience which can be attained only by knowing the real nature of "I" through practice of self-enquiry. The reason why scriptures begin by teaching that five sheaths are not "I", is that in order to practice self-enquiry it is useful for an aspirant to understand intellectually that the "I" which is to be attended to is not the body or any of other adjuncts which are now felt by him to be mixed with the feeling of "I". But since Bhagawan does not want us to fall prey to the misunderstanding that pondering intellectually over the truth that the five sheaths are not "I" is itself the method of negating the five sheaths. He has carefully taught us the method of practice of self-enquiry before revealing to us the conclusion that the five sheaths are not "I". This revolutionary understanding of neti, neti method by Bhagawan contributed a lot in the whole understanding of Advaita and Bhagawan took us to new heights in understanding the method of practice of self-enquiry and in this aspect Bhagawan surpassed Adi Sankara in contributing to the understanding of human consciousness.

*****

Quote

Verse 23: satva bhasika cit kva va etara satta ya hi cit citta ya hi aham

kva va : where (is)

itara: anything else

cit: Consciousness

satva bhasika : the one that Sheds light on the Being, Existence.

Hi Satya cit: Existence is Consciousness

Cit ya hi aham: I alone am Consciousness.

Upadesa Saram Verse 23:

"Because of nonexistence of another consciousness to know that which exists (The reality, Sat, Ulladu) is consciousness (chit, unarvu),that consciousness is itself "we"(The real self)."

Comment:

In the remaining eight verses, Bhagawan reveals more conclusions, which will be useful in helping us to put self-enquiry into practice,but which can be realized through direct experience only when we actually attend to the "I" and there by realize it's true nature. That which exists is real self "I" which shines forth spontaneously when the mind dies. Since this "we"(Self, namay ullam) is the only existence or reality, there cannot exist any consciousness other than it to know it, and hence it is itself the consciousness which knows itself (unarve).Therefore "we"(The reality) are also consciousness (chit). Our existence and the knowledge of our existence are not two different things, but are one and the same reality.

*****

Quote

Verse 24: isha jiva yor vesa dhi bidha. Sat Svabhava yatho vastu kevalam.

isha - jiva - yor: Between The God and individual Self

Vesa dhi bhida: only in appearance [the role played or the body] there is a difference.

Sat Svabhavatah: From the Bhavana of Self. From the Stand point of Self- Truth.

Vastu : The entity

Kevalam: is only one.

Upadesa Saram Verse 24:

"By existing (irukkum) in their real nature which is existence or Sat, God and souls are one substance (vastu). Their adjunct knowledge or adjunct consciousness alone is different."

Comment:
The existence consciousness "I am" is the real nature of both God (Eswara) and of souls (Jivas).But on this "I am" adjuncts or upadhis are superimposed and these adjuncts which are a form of wrong knowledge or ignorance, gives rise to seeming differences which exist between God and soul. The soul feels that he is Kinchigna (Possessing limited knowledge),transient (living for a limited period of time) with limited existence and limited power and he thinks that God is all knowing (Sarvajna),all powerful (omnipotent) all pervading (omniscient) and eternal without birth or death. This is an imagination which exists only in the
outlook of the soul (Jiva Dristi) and not in the outlook of God (Eswara Dristi).

*****

Quote

Verse 25: vesha hanaham svatma darshanam eesha darshanam svatma rupatah

vesha hanatah: devoid of the form, giving up the form

svatma darshanam: One gets a darshan, of vision of the Self.

Isha darshanam: that is God's vision

Svatma Ruptah: As the Self.

Upadesa Saram Verse 25:

"Knowing oneself having given up identity with one's own adjuncts (Upadhis) is itself knowing God, because he shines as oneself as one's own reality (I am)."

Comment:
In Ulladu Narpadu Bhagawan said, "He who sees the real Self, the source of the individual Self, alone is he who has seen God (Here seeing God means being as the "self" whose nature is Godliness), because the "Real Self" which shines forth after the base i.e the individual self has perished--is not other than God."

Since that which exists and shines is one as "I am" is the true nature of God and since it is only one's own adjunct knowledge (Jiva Dristi, Upadhi Unarvu, Vesha dhi) that veils the knowledge of "I am", knowing this "I am", which is one's own real Self, without identity to the adjuncts (Upadhis) is itself knowing God.

*****

Quote

Verse 26: Atma Samstithih svatma darshanam Atma nirdva yad atma nisthata

atma samsthitih : Abidance as the Self.

svatma darshanam: the Vision of one's Self.

Atma nirdvayat: the Self is non-dual.

Atma nishtata: The Firm abidance in the Self.

Upadesa Saram Verse 26:

"Being the self itself is knowing the self, because self is that which is not two.
This is abidance as the reality (Tanmaya Nishta)."

Comment:
Since we do not have two selves, one Self to be known by the other Self, what is called self-knowledge is nothing but the state of being the self i.e the state of abiding "as we really are", as mere existence consciousness "I am" instead of rising as "I am this", "I am that". This state of being is what is called "self abidance" (Atma-Nishta) or "abidance as the reality" (Tanmaya Nishta).

*****

Verse 27: jnana varjita jnana hina cit jnanam asti kim jnatum antaram

ajnana hina: devoid of Ignorance
cit: consciousness
jnana varjita: devoid of knowledge.
jnanam asti : Is there any knowledge
Kim antaram : other than the Self, Consciousness?
Jnatum: To know ?

Upadesa Saram Verse 27:

"The absolute knowledge which is devoid of relative knowledge and ignorance about objects alone is real knowledge. This is Truth because in the state of self experience there is nothing to know other than oneself."

Comment:
The mere consciousness of one's own existence, "I am" which is devoid of both of feeling "I know" and the feeling of "I do not know" alone is true knowledge.

That which knows other than itself is not true knowledge. Since self shines without another for it to know or to make it known,it is true knowledge. Though devoid of knowledge and ignorance which are essentially relative with reference to objects, it is not void--know thus.

*****

Verse 28: kim svarupam iti atma darshane avyaya abhava purna cit sukham

kim svarupam: what is my nature

iti atma darshane: thus inquiring within

avyaya: undecaying, non-decreasing,non-dying

abhava: which was never born

purna cit sukham: Pure Consciousness (which is) Bliss

Upadesa Saram Verse 28:
"Thus enquiring "what is my nature", one finds oneself to be un-decaying and unborn Pure consciousness bliss."

Comment:
If one knows what one's nature is through enquiry (Atma vichara), then what will remain and shine only is the beginning-less, endless, oneness of existence consciousness whose nature is bliss.

*****

Verse 29: Bandha mukti ya atitam param sukham vindati eha jivastu daivakah

bandha mukti ya atitam: that which is beyond "bondage" and "liberation"

parama sukham: that Supreme Bliss [Sukham: a Stationary kind of Stillness/ Being]

jivastu: in this jiva

daivakam: the God or Divine.

29: Bandha mukti ya atitam param sukham vindati eha jivastu daivakah
bandha mukti ya atitam: that which is beyond "bondage" and "liberation"
parama sukham: that Supreme Bliss [Sukham: a Stationary kind of Stillness/ Being]
jivastu: in this jiva
daivakam: the God or Divine.

Upadesa Saram Verse 29:

"biding in this state of self, having attained supreme bliss, which is devoid of bondage and liberation amounts to abiding in God. When one enjoys the bliss which is not of this world, he is as divine as God and in such a state there are no differences like Jiva (Individual soul) and Eswara (God)."

Comment by the author:

When we enquire into the one who feels that he is in bondage, the ever liberated one (Real Self) alone remains as unequivocal truth,since the thought of bondage and liberation cannot remain there. The only service we can render to God is to cease rising as an individual (Ego) and there by refrain by making it necessary for God to run to our rescue to serve us out of his all merciful attitude. One who is established in self has no separative feeling with the God and hence he is not other than God, the one supreme reality. God resides in him and his actions are actions of God.

Verse 30: aham apetakam nija vibanakam mahad idam tapo ramana vag iyam

iyam ramana vak: this is the statement of Ramana
aham apetakam: devoid of the "I" feeling/identification
idam: this
mahad tapah: Great Penance
nija vibhanakam: is the revealer of the Self.

Upadesa Saram Verse 30:

"This self-enquiry which is devoid of "I-am-the-body" feeling, is the great penance which reveals the "nature of Self". This is the Truth as spoken by Bhagawan Ramana."

Comment by the author:

The state of non-rising of ego which is the outcome of doing self-enquiry without any identity to non-self which reveals the nature of Self is great penance says Bhagawan Ramana.

Om Sri Ramanarpanamastu.

*****

Printed in the USA
CPSIA information can be obtained
at www.ICGtesting.com
LVHW080316011123
762685LV00005B/644

9 781494 205515